DREAMWINDS

a book of poetry by
Stephen Brooke

Arachis Press 2011

To sleep: perchance to dream

This is a book of dreams: dreams of love, dreams of darkness, dreams of life and death. Dream with me through these pages, through these poems.

©2011 Stephen Brooke

All rights reserved. The text, art and design of this publication are the copyrighted work of Stephen Brooke and may not be reproduced nor transmitted in any form without the express written permission of the author or the publisher, other than short quotes for review purposes.

ISBN: 978-1-937745-03-5

Arachis Press
4803 Peanut Road
Graceville, FL 32440
http://arachispress.com

My Songs

This soul's a place of shadows,
My songs are lights held high;
Illuminating empty corners,
I seek to glimpse what lies beyond.

This soul's a place of echoes,
My songs resound within:
The pebbles cast into dark wells
To test uncertain depths below.

An Age Ago

There was a sea, a nameless, ice-bound sea,
and we were there; in some forgotten age,
I held you close upon its ancient shore.

I brought the prizes of primeval hunts;
across an empty glacial land I came
to lay before you soft luxurious pelts.

Do you remember star-filled nights we met,
among the shadowed forest hills, to pledge
eternal love beneath a sky still new?

A little while we shared in that cold time
when man was young; yet, there we lived and died
and loved, an age ago, when you were mine.

Aubade

The remnants of these stars
fade as the pale night blooms,
the scented cereus
and jasmine, must with dawn.

As moth on silent wing
so was I drawn to seek
the perfumed doors of you.
So was I drawn to taste

each nectared star that bloomed
more fragrantly above.
Sing to the sky, my sun,
with all dawn's rose-cloud carols.

You are the morning song;
light plays adagios
along the curve of day,
among those remnant stars.

Morning Forest

Awaking in the mist, still all around,
That rises late at night, and clings the ground,
The forest, looking east, prepares to doff
The dark, her now unneeded gown shrugged off,
To bathe in golden dawn, whose first faint ray
Has brought the promise of another day.

As bird song greets the morn from woodland eaves,
And slender shafts of sunlight pierce the leaves,
The last of night has slipped away to sleep
Beneath the trees, hid there in shadow deep:
Retreats the growing glow of dawn can't reach,
The shelter of the ancient oak and beech.

The forest is content to only be;
Reborn each day, she has no memory,
But shining as it ever has before,
The rising sun becomes a thousand more
That sparkle now, reflected in the dew;
Its promise kept, dawn's brought the day anew.

Yucatan

I dream a dream of jungle green,
The calls of birds of Yucatan;
The crumbling stone, the broken throne,
The cities once built up by man
Stand empty now, in Yucatan.

In forests deep the ruins sleep,
Forgotten, buried in their mounds;
I see the priests, the savage feasts,
Where once were sacred temple grounds:
All vanished, lost beneath the mounds.

Dreamwinds
a night journey in three cantos

I.

Awakening, I sense a shudder:
Silent wings above the city,
Beating slowly through the night
In rhythm to the dreaming dark.

Here, angels who have lost their way
Seek solace in an earthly exile,
Reaching out to know men's souls,
To soft bespeak the senseless sleepers.

They are haunted by the hungers
Of unnumbered nights undreaming,
Of uncounted lifetimes' yearnings,
Dreams unborn, undreamt, unfinished.

Wandering this mortal maze,
Through shadowed streets they stalk tomorrow:
Dreams of death, the death of dreams,
And worlds that have failed and fled.

cont.

Dreamwinds *continued*

II.

Now madness rides the wings of night,
As dark winds toss men's sleeping souls
Down endless chasms of despair
That bound hell's bleak forbidding border.

There, they dance the dance of dream
In empty temples, ghost-lit ruins;
Music trilled by unseen pipers
Rises to a starless sky.

cont.

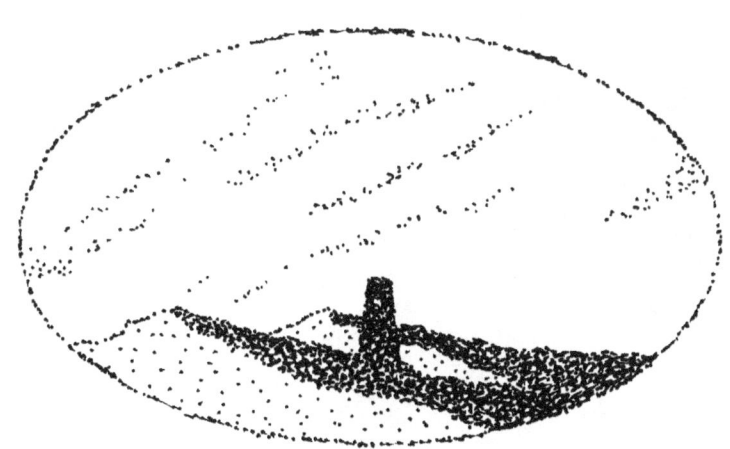

Dreamwinds *continued*

Relentless rhythm holds our hearts,
A thousand throbbing drums in time,
Seducing through the doors of death
To taste of fruit grown sweet with darkness.

Both my eyes are become blind,
For one sees nothing, one sees all;
A glimpse into eternity
Has filled my soul with emptiness.

III.

And still the darkened city dreams
All through the sterile starless night,
With outcast angels hovering,
Those beggars from the streets of heaven.

Dogs of darkness gnaw the bones
Of our discarded yesterdays;
Remembered rhythms of my heart
The winds bring echoed in their howls.

cont.

Dreamwinds *continued*

Have I awakened yet again
To feel those wings, now all about me?
Dawn draws near, hounds howl your last;
Your pack has worried night enough.

While killers coolly stroll the ways
Between these worlds known to dream,
Returning stars have found my sky
To fade, in turn, before the dawn.

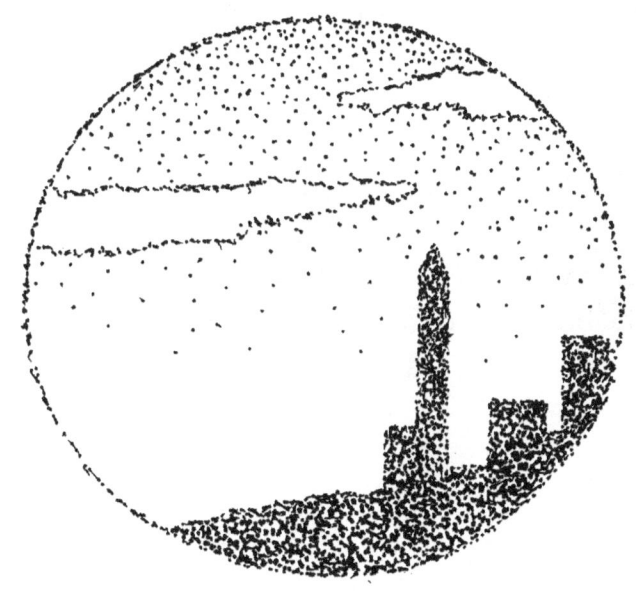

The Sleeping God

In a wilderness of peaks and vast high falls,
Lies one sleeping, ancient and titanic;
There have long the brooding, dark volcanic
Mountains ringed him all about, impris'ning walls.

He, at times, stirs heavily, still bound by slumber,
Dreaming of deep fires that will consume
Rocky fences, ever slow; his doom
Surely ended after ages without number.

Will he, that day, waking there in solitude,
Rise once more to stride like some young god,
Go forth, lightning helmed and earthquake shod,
To a world since grown old, his reign renewed?

Or, in wonder gazing, shake a mighty head,
Then steal from the kingdom of his youth,
To seek limbos where he may know ruth:
Ruling in the Blessed Isles, among the dead?

The Towers of Atlantis

Then, I lived, though mem'ry's faded,
On an isle, with towers high crowned:
Fair Atlantis, of days olden.
In lands long lost, that now lie drowned,
I once dallied in the golden
Gardens where my care was banished,
By the spreading gingko shaded;
All that world has now vanished.

Then, I was content, if humble,
And in peace I made my dwelling
Where the fragrant flowing fountains
Sang, in secret valleys welling.
On those sea-girt, mighty mountains
Stood the high and haughty towers,
Fallen now, for towers crumble,
Bowing down to greater powers.

Now, we leave such ways behind us
In our haste to meet tomorrow,
Building once more, ever higher.
Souls discarded, to our sorrow,
Tossed to any glib-tongued buyer,
And the truth best left unspoken:
For, as then, a day will find us,
Yet again, with towers broken.

Ancient, Our Love

I have sought you through shining galaxies;
Your voice I've heard borne on an alien breeze.
In an empty land, I once glimpsed your face,
Among the ruins of some elder race.
We have embraced on the cold plains of Mars,
And made love by the light of unknown stars.

A sun's first dawning has seared our eyes;
Over molten mountains, we witnessed its rise.
The stars by their billions burst forth in fire,
And life began its long climb from the mire.
On countless planets, through endless ages,
You and I have turned Eternity's pages.

We have awaited the coming of night
To weary worlds of dying light,
And heard a despairing people cry;
They perished beneath the darkening sky.
Then watched one last fragile blossom grow
By the gleam of a pale rising moon's final glow.

As suns of many hues colored our days,
We dallied along the jewel-paved ways
Of rainbow cities where sages converse
Loftily of the universe;
You laughed at their small, smug pretenses,
Having learned to trust not even your senses.

cont.

Ancient, Our Love *continued*

Through twists of time, we may have met
On airless plateaus, or watched twin suns set,
Reflecting dimly on some black-iced shore;
We know these brief moments, and no more.
Ancient, our love is and ancient our fate:
Destined ever to seek our mate.

If we should meet under hurtling moons,
Where shadows form enigmatic runes,
We'll tarry a while, yet then must part,
To wander once more, with yearning heart,
Isles scattered across a starry sea,
Until we are one in infinity.

In Dreams

In dreams, I have the love you keep from me;
You flow into me with the tide of night.
In dreams, I find a love that can not be;
Yet, with all of my soul, I wish it might.

In dreams, there is no other at your side;
I feel your heartbeat singing in the dark.
In dreams, I would forever more abide,
As waking brings realities too stark.

In dreams, I take your willing hand in mine,
But come unwelcome dawn you slip away.
In dreams, I may drink deeply of your wine;
The bitter lees, I swallow with the day.

So, sleep I shall seek ever, for it seems
That I shall hold you never, save in dreams.

The Dance of Days

Should life not be a dance
To music from our souls;
Should we not seek to laugh,
Forsaking empty goals?
Each new day is a chance,
We all know whose bell tolls.

So drink the wine of life,
So sing the songs of pleasure;
We'll never count what's left
Nor take the time to measure,
And shun the ways of strife,
The laying up of treasure.

Although our days be few,
Delight in every one;
Fill each with happiness,
With laughter and with sun,
Rememb'ring it is true
That life will wait for none.

These Little Things

I'm not a poet of these little things,
Such as already seem to fill my days,
Content to tell of life with folded wings,
Of how the garden grows and simple ways.

No, I would sing of wonders, worlds far,
The lands that lie beneath another sky;
Of planets circling some dim distant star
Where, unnamed, through its azure lights they fly.

Or of great towering romance I'd rhyme,
Mad dark desires, obsession burning deep,
And passions binding lovers through all time
With souls too full of fevered dream to sleep.

Then seeking more, I may, in days to come,
Yet find these little things that so please some.

Garden Song

Within my garden, take repose,
Of all the flowers, fairest Rose;
There, in the cool and fragrant shade,
You may rest, my lovely maid.

The lily and the hyacinth
Must bow before your radiance;
Amid such beauty, yours alone
Should all reverence be shown.

cont.

Garden Song *continued*

Among the gay, bold blooms I'll lurk,
As though I were a bee at work,
And gather scented nectar there
From the blossom of your hair.

So none disturb us, I shall set
A lock upon the garden gate;
Allowing time to pass us by,
As the flowers, you and I.

I Can Not Turn Away

There are some who call me fool
To allow my heart to rule,
But there is naught else I can do;
I can not turn away from you.

Empty, life would ever be
If I spurned your love for me;
My foolishness should be well known
Then, surely, were I all alone.

So I give them my rebuff,
Those who say I'm wrong to love,
For there is naught else I can do;
I can not turn away from you.

In Love's Service

Though oft I wear Love's livery,
No mistress of mine shall she be.
Of Love's bonds I will be free
To sup on life and have my fill,
To take my pleasures where I will;
I'll remain my own man still.

So, if Love's praises I may sing,
Know that my words mean not a thing;
They are birds that take to wing.
They bear sweet songs to whom they might
And, leaving naught to mark their flight,
Are away and out of sight.

I'll stay not long in Love's service,
Only a while, to have her kiss.
Then I'll go, rememb'ring this:
She welcomes back all former men,
However long it may have been,
Come to share her gifts again.

Love's School

I'd heard of love and laughed at he
Who chanced to catch this malady:
The semblance of insanity;
An ailment cured by no pill,
It clouds its victims' minds until
Mere men abandon wit and will.

Now, never having been one such,
I had not thought overly much
Of love and did not know its touch;
And, ever counting myself wise,
I laughed at all its sweetest lies
Or that I saw in girls' eyes.

The truth, I should have understood,
Is love brings forth both ill and good:
It damns and blesses those it would.
So, know then, I was once a fool
But am become love's willing tool;
I've learned the lessons of love's school.

In Praise of Love

I know of nothing more complete than love;
It speaks the very essence of existence
And all the vast infinities of distance
Found in the softest whispers of a dove.

A kiss holds secrets men seek all their days,
Philosophers and fools alike have learned;
From time's first tick, each human heart has yearned
For love, and love's the god to which each prays.

cont.

In Praise of Love *continued*

I sing in praise of love, yet I still fear
To reach for love today, letting tomorrow
Bring its embrace of ecstasy and sorrow;
Such hesitation fades when you are near.

None know the future, save the Lord above,
So with the earthly chorus I shall raise
Another hopeful voice to sing love's praise
And ever seek to be complete in love.

Once

Once, I fell in love
and, falling, broke my heart;
each time I thought it mended,
it once more came apart.
Need it be bound and bandaged
till it no longer feels;
allowed to sleep a season,
lest it never heals?

Once, I was in love
and, loving, spoke my heart;
left it undefended,
a target for each dart.
Such wounds I will bear gladly;
they speak not of defeat,
for hearts can not be hidden
without their loss complete.

Once, I fell in love
and, falling, broke my heart.
In time, it may be mended;
then, perhaps, I'll start
to fear not once more falling,
to trust again my wings,
and, guarding not my heart,
to hope for all love brings.

Shadow

Are we meant to know happiness,
To live and laugh beneath blue skies,
Or does day but hold back the dark
That turns all of our hopes to lies?

Each new-found joy, each pleasure seems
To give way, in its turn, to pain;
As every man a shadow casts,
So loss will surely follow gain.

Room

Come night, I will too often go
To gaze beyond my window's glow;
Into another realm I peer,
Upon a world that I fear,
Into the darkness I must know.

I am, perhaps, drawn from a book,
From quiet study in some nook,
Or from the comfort of my bed
To that dark glass I'm once more led,
I'm once more called to blindly look.

The shelter of my empty room,
The safety of its changeless gloom,
Speaks to me of all that I lack,
The fears that ever hold me back,
But none can live within a tomb.

I rest my head, I close my eyes,
I tell myself my newest lies,
Yet night brings hidden thoughts to me,
Temptation whispers *come and be*;
The darkness calls, no one replies.

Fortress

He has no faith in person nor in thing,
And trusting nothing that he has not seen,
Believes that earthly knowledge makes him king:
Respecting only logic, cold and keen.

The curses and the blessing brought by love,
And passions of the soul he has not felt.
He has no need of man nor god above;
The ice within his heart will never melt.

A fortress raised temptation can not take,
Like rocky crags, all sin his mind repels,
For frozen far too long to ever break,
Such ice remains hard in the hottest hells.

The touch of death, like other men, he'll know,
But he'll have lived but little ere he go.

Pride

I have worshiped at the altar
of pride, the greatest sin,
sin of the great, or those who would
believe themselves to be.

I was but a slave who thought
I had set myself free,
deluded, drunk on life's sweet wine,
this world's heady din.

Pride held up its empty mirror
and I, a fool, was flattered
to see myself so nobly stand
against oppressive God.

I had done no more than choose
another master's rod.
That mirror holds no more deceptions;
with me, it now lies shattered.

Some Never Sing

Some never seem to set their voices free;
The words go lacking music all their days.
They are content to plod their prosey ways,
At ease with only what they know to be,
When they might run on paths of poetry.
Though others' voices lift to God in praise,
They have no music more than donkeys' brays;
They dare not dream beyond the fields we see.

For all of those who never learn to sing
Remain within the limits of their bond,
Not knowing of the music life could bring,
The melody of each day newly dawned.
They must limp on and never take to wing,
Without a song to carry them beyond.

Look, Sometime

Look, sometime, beyond the walls
You have built up and hear the calls
Of shining worlds that await
One bold enough to trust his fate:
To use his life in search of pleasures,
Reaching forth to grasp Earth's treasures.

Labor not without avail
In causes that are bound to fail,
But cast aside self-made indentures,
Seeking after new adventures:
Find fresh purpose every day
In what may chance to come your way.

Free Your Songs

Sit not small within yourself,
Smash those walls raised all around;
Loose your heavy-handed poems
   On any who deny them.

Do not be the silenced voice,
Loath to whisper in the night,
Lest you wake those sleeping secrets
   Long thought best kept concealed.

Heed not cautious, empty men
Whose words urge you to restraint;
Free the songs you have imprisoned,
   That you might dream new dreams.

All

Each heart yearns to be free
And slave, all in the same;
To hazard chance and choice,
But never face the blame.
To soar to unknown heights
And, yet, not take the fall;
At once, to play it safe
But still to have it all.

Uncertainty

Uncertainty's the lot of man;
in truth, it is a gift of sorts.
For some brief while we live in light
and darkness, if it lies beyond,
is best kept hidden from our sight.

To clearly see our destined ends,
to brood upon them all the days,
could be no blessing to mankind.
Such knowledge surely will bring madness:
it is better to be blind.

Forget the Dead

Sing not your songs of yesterday;
No, only say
Those things that must be said.
Let come what may:
Forget the dead.

Know all that is will ever be;
Too soon we see
What lies in wait ahead.
Set time past free:
Forget the dead.

Ghosts in Gray

Beneath the fading stars they pass,
too dim for mortal sight,
Shadows moving in the mist,
before dawn's first pale light.
They have arisen rank on rank,
to rejoin the fight,
And a lonely fife is playing 'Dixie'
somewhere in the night.

From a hundred battlefields
where rebel blood once flowed,
From the ruined ramparts
where the rebel color showed,
Still true to their defeated cause
and to their soldiers' code,
Ghosts in gray go marching down
a dusty southern road.

cont.

Ghosts in Gray *continued*

A call to arms has wakened them
from solitary sleep;
Their exiled brothers they have joined,
with pledges yet to keep.
And though no man is left to mourn,
no woman left to weep,
They did not lie forgotten,
Southern mem'ries run too deep.

They have but a few hours here
before they fade away,
Departing from this world
with the coming of the day.
May they find the peace at last
that they deserve, I pray,
And as they pass by, I salute
those gallant ghosts in gray.

The Song of the Sword

The song of the shining sword, I sing,
The song of a bird with a bright steel wing;
I sing of blows that make blades ring,
The life it has, the death it will bring.

My tales of time-lost battles I tell,
The sieges where great cities fell;
Of men who fought bravely and well,
The many souls sent down to hell.

To music made by clashing shields,
The sword sings over many fields;
A scythe Death unrelenting wields:
Men's lives, the crop his reaping yields.

I watch by the light of a blood-red moon,
Where broken ramparts rise in ruin;
The cold wind carries a song of doom
As armies march to the ancient tune.

cont.

The Song of the Sword *continued*

Before the sword, each nation falls;
It brings Achaeans against Troy's walls.
Barbarians plunder Roman halls;
The mighty end their days as thralls.

The sword cares naught for prideful powers
That gather wealth and build high towers.
It throws them down as mankind cowers;
They lie forgotten beneath the flowers.

So, I shall sing the song of the sword,
Of that which ever is man's lord;
A song arising from discord,
For we march still to the song of the sword.

Exeunt Omnes

It's true that life is but a stage;
from page to page and age to age
we play a part and then we go,
as others carry on the show.
   Exeunt omnes.

Our way is scripted from the womb,
from room to room down to the tomb;
the author ever has made certain
his plays include a final curtain.
   Exeunt omnes.

We act a role before the throng,
from right to wrong, from weak to strong;
remember that this show will run
long after our small part is done.
   Exeunt omnes.

The Gaze of the Cat

The beast has broken loose
and, hungry, prowls the dark.
It ever seeks to fix
its shining eye on me.
Quickly, hide, my soul;
avoid the gaze of the cat.
Those jaws, once clamped, would shake
the spirit like a toy.

Against the Night

I have seen our future:
Our future dreams no dreams.
I see a nightmare world
Where the Morlock screams;
A night is closing on us,
An end to all our schemes.

Man hides away his soul,
It's value he denies;
He seeks out oracles
That comfort him with lies,
Performing pointless tasks
Under darkening skies.

We, like thoughtless children,
Wait atop a slide,
Till Fate's unyielding push
Starts our downward ride
Into the night that swallows
Up our trifling pride.

Will we ask at the end
Who stands against the night?
We will not find one hero
To guard the dying light.
Night comes ever closer;
None stops eternal night.

Forgotten Gods

I am the priest of long forgotten gods,
Who ruled the world when it was yet young;
    Give praise, give praise!
I offer sacrifice at broken altars,
Where once the ancient solemn hymns were sung;
    The off'rings blaze!

I honor still the elder deities,
At cobwebbed shrines since fallen in decay;
    Let incense burn!
I am the priest of those our fathers knew,
For they but sleep and have not gone away;
    The gods return!

In Earth's Last Days

In Earth's last days, the senile sun
stands dim against a darkened sky;
there stars, grown few, yet palely glow
above a world soon to die,
a place of dust and bitter seas
that cold and gray and shrunken lie.

Man ventures not the pallid light,
no beast now wanders ruined plains;
still, shadow shields those that would dream
the dreams of cold and bloodless brains,
of ages when all Earth is theirs,
a time when only darkness reigns.

The last of men survive yet hidden,
delving after dying fires:
worms that crawl Earth's lifeless body.
Their despair feeds strange desires,
given vent in caverns deep;
at time's bleak end, mankind expires.

cont.

In Earth's Last Days *continued*

Unto the chill, forsaken orb
come ancient ones, unknown to man,
from limbos dark, beyond the stars,
grown old before our race began;
these last days of Earth call gods
across a universe's span.

Wielding mad, demonic powers,
they now rule the twilit land
as lords of wastes and desolation,
whose dark towers hill-top stand
where sluggish, leaden rivers flow
through empty realms of ice and sand.

The gods abide here, for a while,
in castles built by long-dead kings;
enthroned within the crumbling keeps,
they wait on all that nightfall brings
and, weary, brood upon their fate:
to live beyond the end of things.

A World Dies

In depths beyond depths, lie stars hidden
Eye of man shall never view,
And there the planets fly forgotten
Through vermilion lights, and blue.
While demons, bound where they are bidden,
Soar across chaotic skies
To lands long lifeless, realms grown rotten;
As all things, a world dies.

Foul towers thrust decaying fingers,
Clawing toward diminished suns;
There wizards seek within their dreams,
Each carried where his drugged mind runs.
Despair awaits he who yet lingers,
Chambered high above the plain,
To brood on fate, for its seems
That his creator is insane.

cont.

A World Dies *continued*

On tumbled tors, vines twist, they bloom,
Corrupt, beset by leprous blight;
They bud forth cancered, cold, pale petals
By a dim orb's azure light:
The flowers on a world's tomb
For, spirit gone, a shell abides
With poisoned air that tastes of metals,
Ashen seas that know no tides.

The waning lamps yet wind their ways
To glimmer over empty land
Grown dark with time and dark with fate,
Where monstrous growths of fungi stand.
While endless pass the twilit days,
Long nights when fear stands black and stark;
In shadow, shambling things await
The coming of a greater dark.

The Wind That's Never Still

Before a sun that will not rise,
A dawn that can not be,
My soul's a storm-lost ship that flies
Across the shoreless sea.
I and the wind and the broken skies
Through eternity;
There is no man to hear my cries,
No god to hear my plea.

I sail a vessel of despair,
Stripped of hope and will:
My world's bones have been laid bare
By the wind that's never still.

There's no rebirth for what has died;
Empty I stand at last,
All love discarded in my pride,
All feeling, ages past.
Night forever at my side,
Cold and black and vast,
I'm borne upon some random tide,
Damned, alone, outcast.

cont.

The Wind That's Never Still *continued*

Darkness shakes the shadowed sails;
I watch them silent fill
And curse the wind that never fails,
The wind that's never still.

The Triumph of the Night

My soul is clad in armor,
hard and cold as steel;
my heart is strongly shielded
so it can not feel.
Armor forged of hatred,
armor forged of might,
armor for a soldier
in the legions of the night.

My soul is closely guarded,
behind a fortress wall;
I watch from piled-high ramparts
and await night's fall.
Walls built up of sorrow,
walls that shut all light,
stand unbreachable
about the children of the night.

cont.

The Triumph of the Night *continued*

My soul is shod in iron;
my booted heavy tread
sounds empty down the haunted
dwellings of the dead.
Boots for trampling under,
bloodied in the fight;
boots made for the marchings
of the armies of the night.

My soul is cloaked in shadow,
black as starless sky;
I wait enrobed of darkness
and watch the future die.
Shadow filled with silence,
shadow void of light,
my eternal witness
to the triumph of the night.

When Death Comes

When Death comes, I will be here,
I'll take his cold hand without fear;
I've lived a life with no regrets
For might-have-beens or losing bets.

When Death comes, I will not flinch,
I'll not step back a single inch,
Nor claim I wasn't given time
To fully live this life of mine.

When Death comes, I will be free,
I'll fly where my fate carries me:
An actor who has played his role
With all his fire, with all his soul.

What Never Was

The days have come, the days have gone,
The days have carried us on and on;
All we can do is let them go,
For now is all we know.

Each of us has his own regrets,
The misplaced dreams, the misplaced bets —
What never was, what never will,
And love that lingers still.

The Doors of Spring

Let us now open the doors of tomorrow
and find there a springtime to this, our dark winter;
gone are the long yesterdays of refusal
that ever have brought us these cold ways and sorrow.

Sing of the season, of summer returning,
of our new beginning, and seeds to be planted.
Life is reborn with the young year's arrival;
the darkness disperses, the pascal fire's burning.

No more must we abide living by measures;
too long we've persisted in such self-denial.
Worlds await us, the red bud is blooming;
the doors are thrown open to all springtime's pleasures.

The House of My Heart

For you, I built the house of my heart,
with all my skill and every art;
upon the mountain did I build
and roofed it with dreams unfulfilled.

This house is now but stones piled high,
my roof a span of empty sky,
for in these rooms, alone, I dwell,
ensorcelled here by my own spell,

caught up in coils of endless yearning,
each chance of healing lethe spurning.
I'll ever linger, one apart;
I'll ever haunt the house of my heart.

Some Summer Lost

Evening creeps into the day,
Stealing all the light away;
Colors slipping softly gray
Are touched, now, by one last ray.
Fleeting, in the final glow,
Memories may start to grow:
Dreams once dreamed we yet half-know,
Sunsets faded long ago.

There is a past for which I find my soul still longs
When distant comes the murmur of forgotten songs
To open wide the gates of time; then, winging free,
I fly the shadowed valleys of my memory,
As echoes of some summer lost in yesterday
Repeat their stories yet again and fade away.

Upon a half-remembered course my heart will steer
By the illumination of that other year,
A shining star placed in the sky as guide to me,
Now standing steady, high above the nighted sea;
Until I reach at last my own familiar shore
And come to rest in lands of present day once more.

Dreams Have Wings

We need not stand alone against
   All time may choose to send;
I know how life's uncaring song
Can echo in our ears o'er long:
Regrets become the ghosts that throng
   Too closely at day's end.

Come with me to a distant land,
   Come with me far away;
Perhaps down to some harbor side,
A fog-choked port where tall ships ride,
And there allow a chance-met tide
   To bear us where it may.

For dreams have wings to carry us
   Beyond this world's strife;
Away from days like unlit stairs,
The long nights filled with faceless cares.
We'll leave our meaningless affairs,
   Our weariness with life.

cont.

Dreams Have Wings *continued*

Each memory will lose itself,
   Caught by the winds of time,
Till all the past has blown away,
The scattered scraps of yesterday;
Then only our tomorrows stay,
   Unopened casks of wine.

Come with me and we'll find a place,
   A place for you and me;
Across unmeasured miles we'll fly,
Across the seas to lands that lie
Beneath an ever cloudless sky,
   And there we can be free.

I Shall Still Know You

When the stars shift from their places,
Making constellations new,
Though we may then wear other faces,
I shall still know you.

Different suns may shine above,
New worlds turn beneath our feet;
But time can not undo the love
That destines we shall meet.

And when your soul's eternal songs
Awake in me this love yet true,
My guide can be a heart that longs,
For I shall still know you.

Old Cat

Old Tom, asleep on the mat,
Dreams of mice, juicy and fat,
Lively, yet easy to catch;
These are dreams of an old cat.

Old man, asleep in his chair,
Dreams of one, laughing and fair,
Who slipped away long ago;
Dreaming, old men, old cats, share.

A Song of the Setting Sun

There is a song,
Sung in the evening,
Sung to the setting sun;
A song sung to children grown sleepy,
A song sung to stars
Stole into the sky.

There is a song,
Sung by the breeze,
Sung on a soft summer eve;
The song of the whip-poor-will calling,
The song of the night
Come carrying dreams.

Last Call

Last call, gents, get yours now,
as we'll be closing soon;
fill those glasses, one more round,
before you head for home.
Last call, gents, what will it be?
The hour is upon us;
toast farewell and then you must
go out into the dark.

Drink up, gents, it's growing late,
we'll serve no more tonight;
closing time is closing time,
and that we can not change.
Drink up, gents, we have to lock
the doors and douse the lights;
drain your glasses so we may
send you into the dark.

To Darkness

When you grow weary,
When you are alone,
Seek out the darkness;
The darkness remains.
It hears not your voice,
It sees not your face,
But goes not away:
Blessed be darkness.

www.ingramcontent.com/pod-product-compliance
Lightning Source LLC
Chambersburg PA
CBHW020022050426
42450CB00005B/594